FRUITS
COLORING BOOK
For Kids

ERiin

APPLE

BANANA

ORANGE

STRAWBERRY

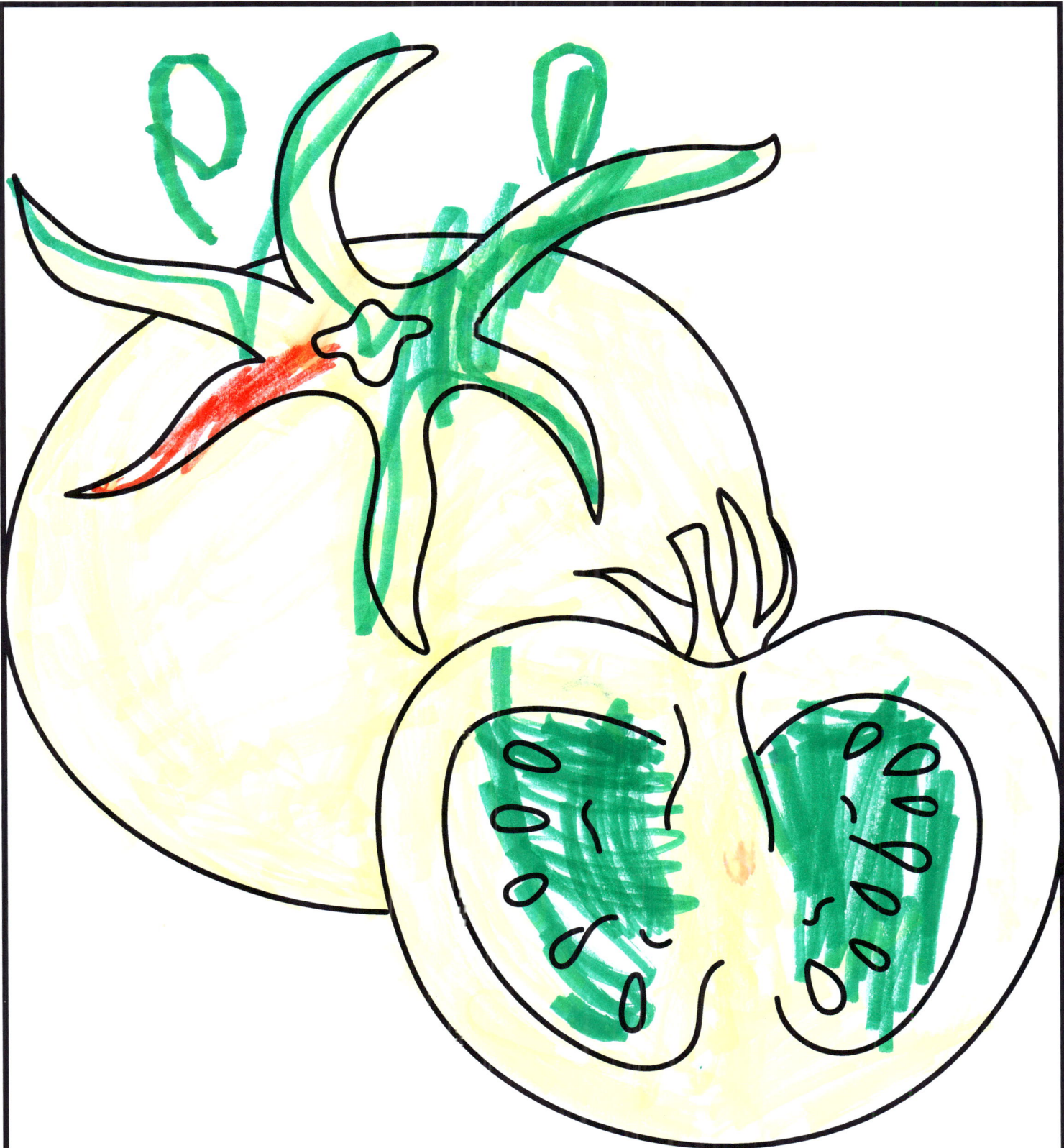

TOMATO

GRAPES

AVOCADO

PINEAPPLE

PEACH

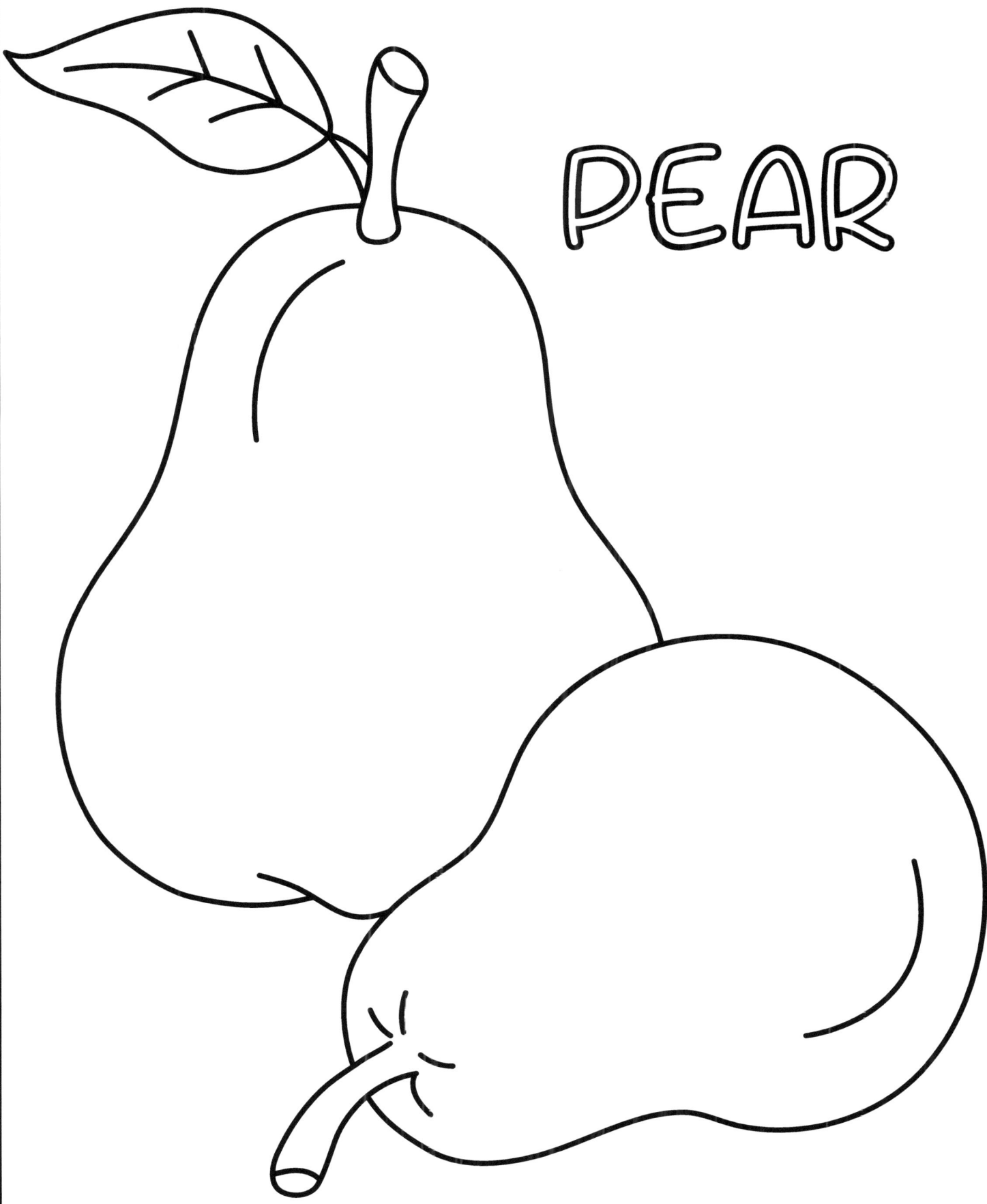

PEAR

APRICOT

WATERMELON

LEMON

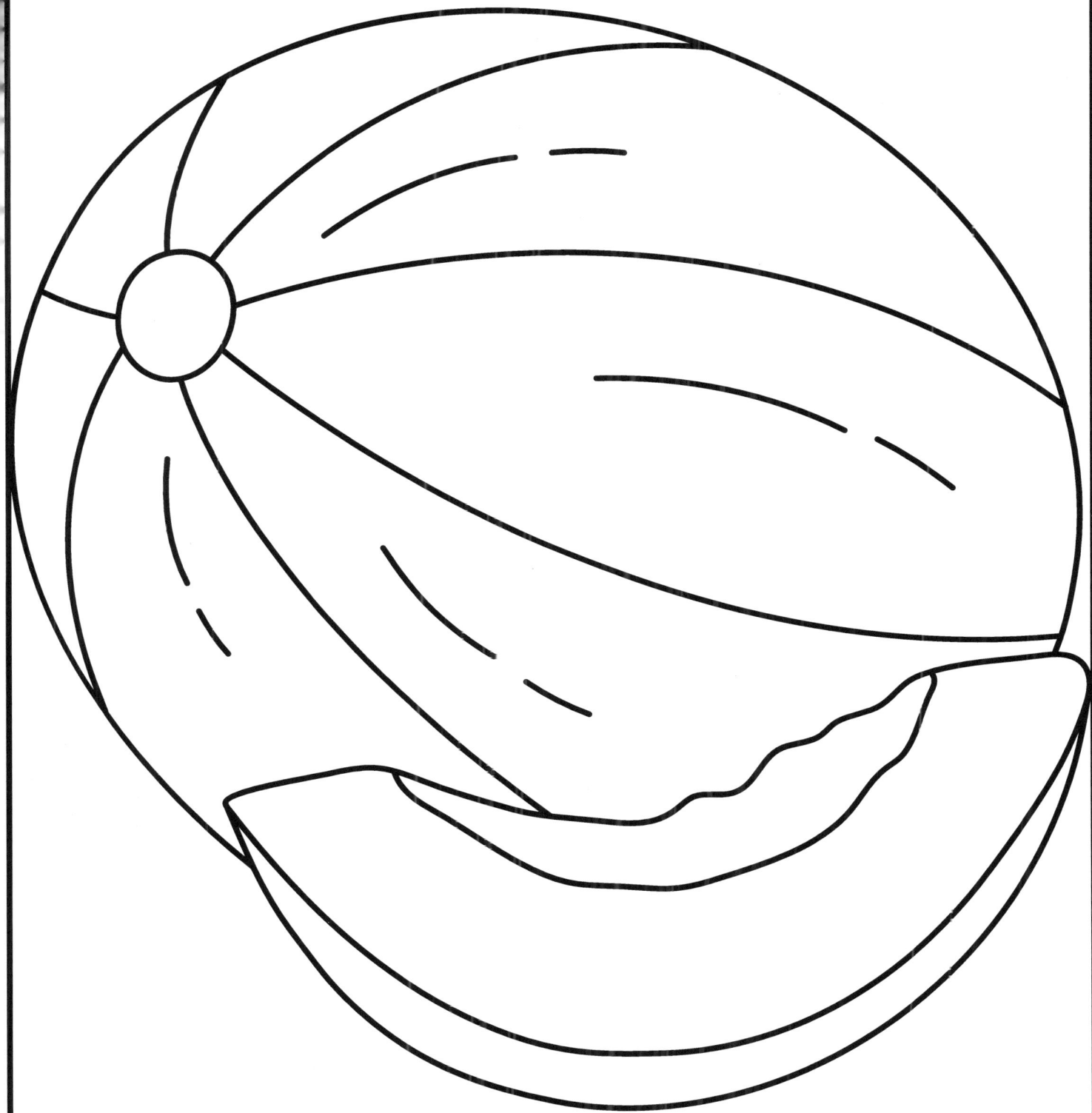

MELON

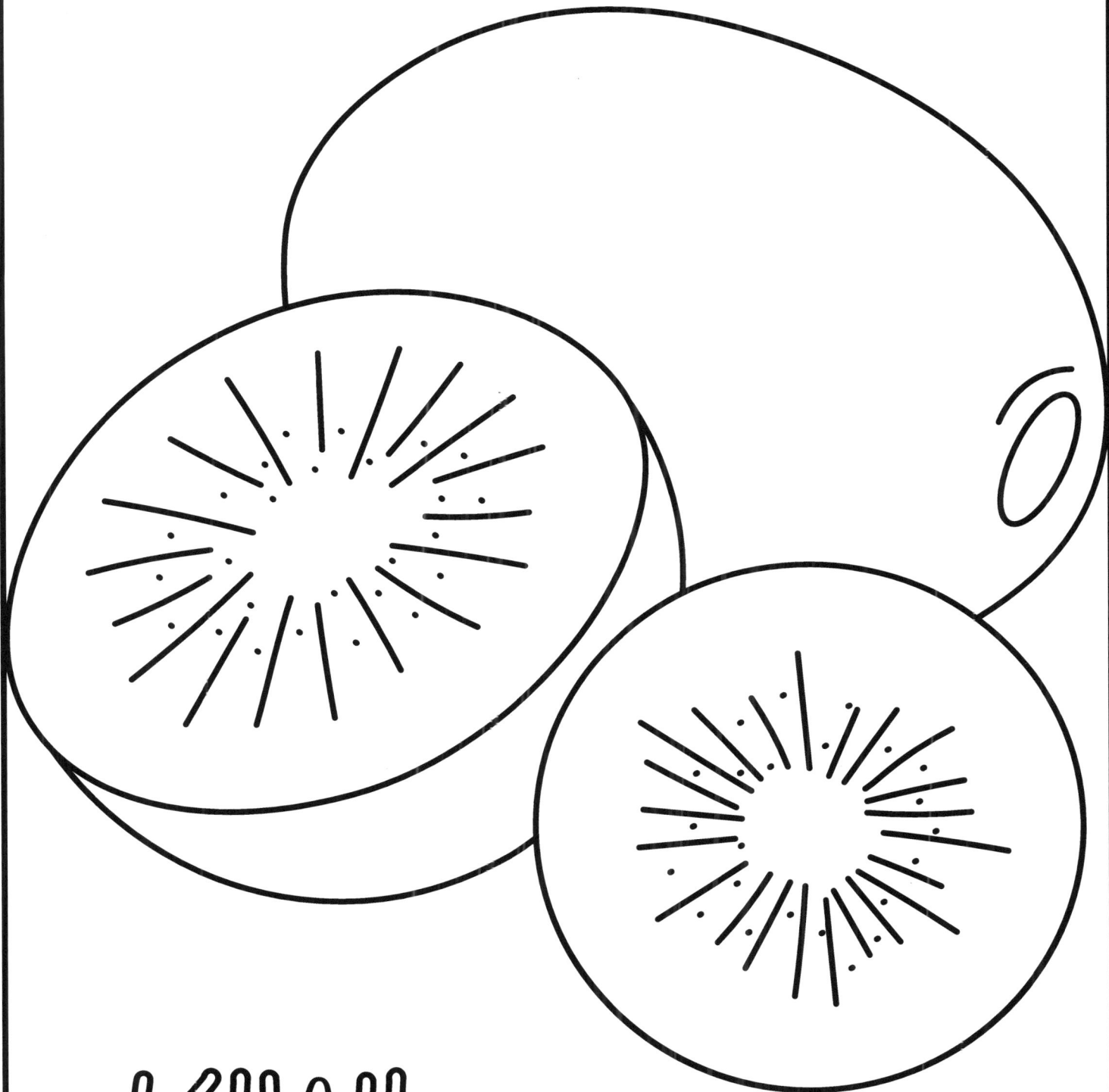

KIWI

MANGO

BLUEBERRIES

PLUM

COCONUT

POMEGRANATE

CHERRY

DATE

FIGS

CARAMBOLA

LYCHEE

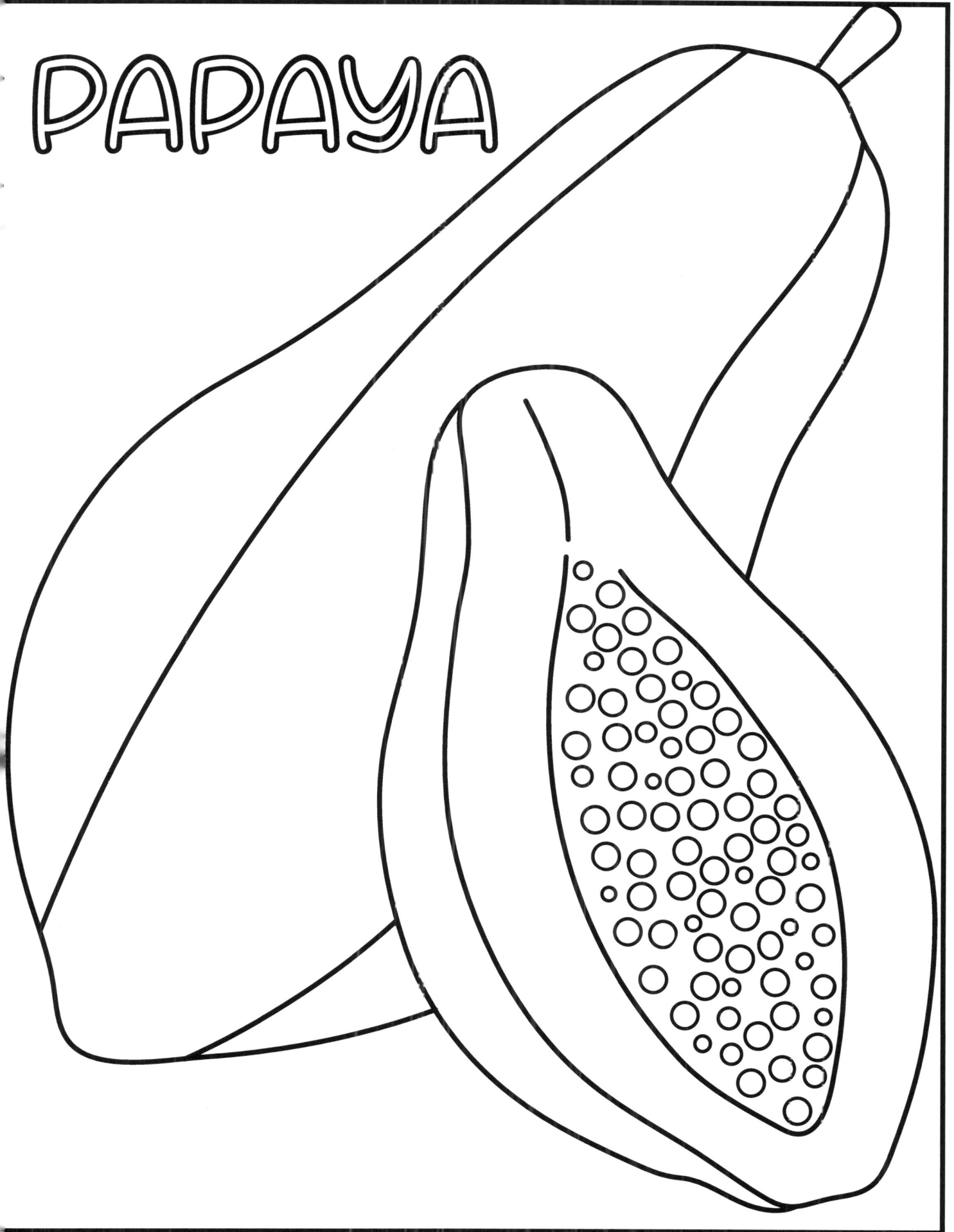

PAPAYA

GUAVA

DRAGON FRUIT

RASPBERRY

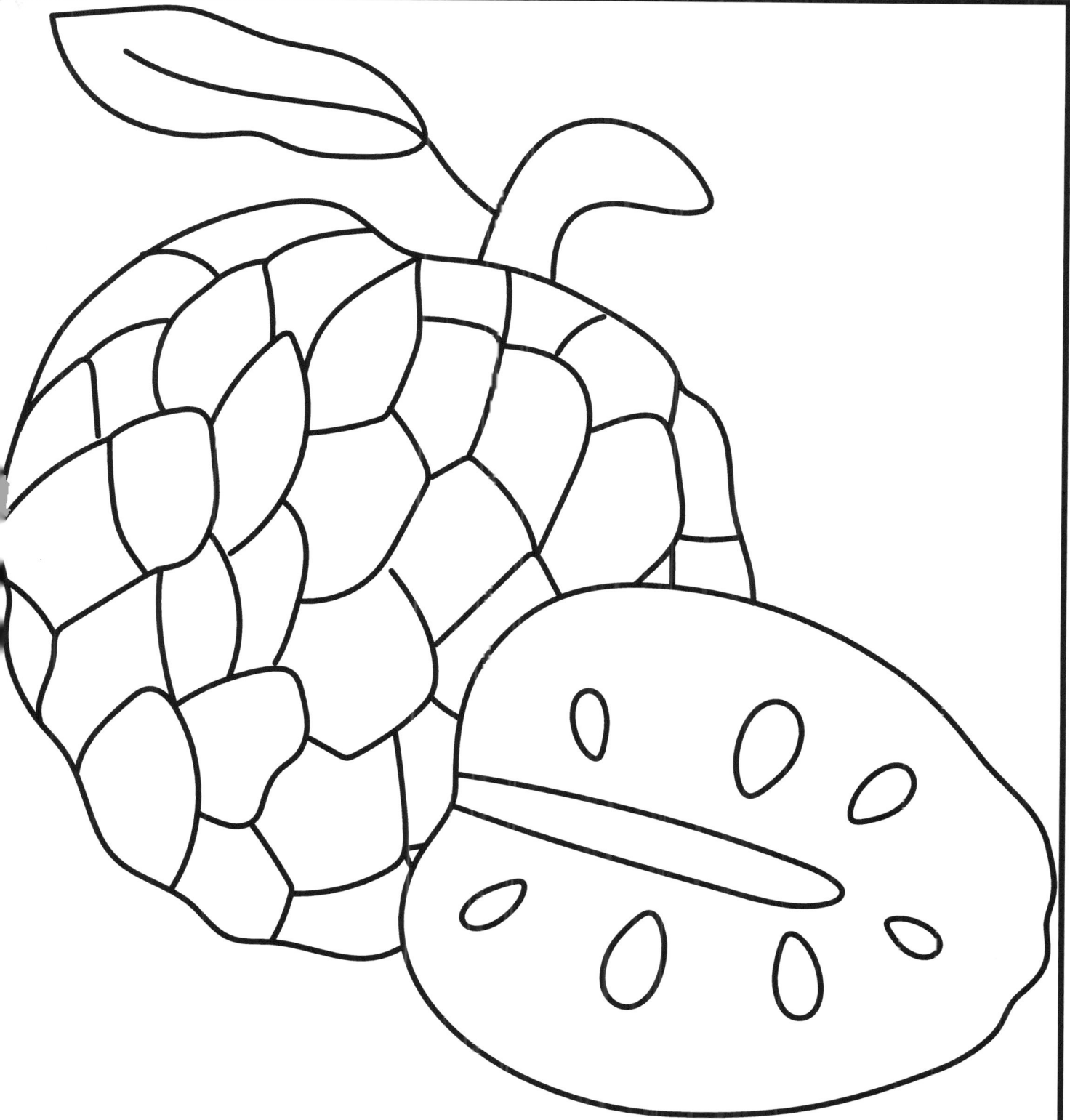

SUGAR APPLE

Manufactured by Amazon.ca
Bolton, ON